Making It! 👍

Artist

DOWN'S SYNDROME ASSOCIATION
Registered Charity
No.1061474

Eleanor Archer

W
FRANKLIN WATTS
LONDON • SYDNEY

Cherry is an artist. She paints, draws and makes prints.

Cherry has won three art competitions. She judges competitions too. Having Down's Syndrome doesn't stop Cherry from doing what she loves.

Cherry has Down's Syndrome which means she finds it harder to learn some everyday skills such as speaking clearly or concentrating. Down's Syndrome is a type of learning difficulty.

Cherry has a busy day ahead. "Do you have an art class at college today?" asks Cherry's mum as they have breakfast together. "Yes, then I'm going to the studio," Cherry tells her.

People with learning difficulties may find it hard to learn to speak clearly. Cherry speaks clearly but sometimes gets tired and has difficulty concentrating on her words.

After breakfast Cherry catches the bus to college. She travels with her friends. "I can't wait for the class today," she says.

Cherry is very independent. She travels on the bus on her own. Some people with learning difficulties may need more support than others.

At college Cherry makes her way to the class. "Back to my screen printing," she thinks to herself.

Cherry paints onto a screen. It is a portrait of Maria, her support assistant.

When Cherry is at college she has a support assistant to help her with the equipment and tools.

Cherry works on her painting. "I hope I don't have a square face like that!" laughs Maria.

"I love your face!" Cherry tells her.

Because Cherry has Down's Syndrome she looks a little different. Her eyes slant and she is not as tall as some people her age.

When the painting is finished,
Cherry dries the paint with a hairdryer.
"To speed it up," she tells Maria.

Next Cherry pushes glue through the screen.
It makes the paint come through the other
side onto the paper.
"Brilliant!" they say to each other.

At lunch time, Cherry meets up with her friends and her boyfriend, Andrew. "It's good to see you," she tells him.

In the afternoon Cherry goes to the art studio. It is run by Gael and her husband. Cherry is having an exhibition of her paintings and has to get ready for it. She chooses which pictures to take. "I like that one," Cherry says to Gael.

Next Cherry packs up the pictures
she is taking to the exhibition.
Each one needs to be carefully wrapped.

Then they look at Cherry's portfolio. "This print is nice, Cherry," says Gael. She makes a note in her file.

Cherry sells her paintings and prints to earn money. Some people with learning difficulties are not able to work and earn their own money. They may need support all the time.

It's time for a break.
Cherry and Gael
relax with a drink.
"How about doing
some work this afternoon?"
Gael suggests.

The art studio is run for people with learning difficulties. The staff who work there support and help all the artists.

Cherry does some work on her painting. "I like the texture of the paint on his face," she says to herself.

Then she does some
clay modelling.
It's very relaxing.
Cherry has had
a long day and
feels tired.

The art studio gives Cherry the opportunity, with support, to use her talent and energy.

"I can't wait for the exhibition next week," Cherry thinks. "All those people looking at my paintings. It's so exciting!"

The following week,
Cherry has displayed
her paintings at the
gallery ready for
the exhibition.

"I am so proud!" Cherry
tells herself happily.

So you want to be an artist?

1. There are lots of different types of art, not just painting – try making a collage or modelling clay.

2. Some people go to art school. But you don't have to go to art school to be a good artist.

3. Collect some of your best work and have an exhibition. Why don't you exhibit at your school?

4. You may need special equipment such as brushes and paints. These can be expensive. See if a local company will sponsor you,

5. Find a place to work. It doesn't have to be a studio, but it should be a place where you can work quietly without being disturbed.

Facts about learning difficulties

- A learning difficulty means a person finds it harder to learn some things. It doesn't mean that they can't learn them.

- There are different types of learning difficulties. Down's Syndrome is a condition that people are born with.

- Some people with learning difficulties may learn to read and write, some may not. Some people may get a job and live on their own, some may need to be looked after. Remember, everyone is different.

How you can help

- Some people with learning difficulties need help. Ask first and listen to the answer, the person may not need help at all!

- A person with learning difficulties may have difficulty speaking clearly. Listen carefully and be patient.

- Talk directly to the person who has the learning difficulty. Don't ask questions through another person.

- Remember, people with learning difficulties like to be treated the same as everyone else!

Addresses and further information

The Down's Syndrome Association
155 Mitcham Road
London
SW17 9PG
www.downs-syndrome.org.uk

Mencap
123 Golden Lane
London, EC1Y 0RT
www.mencap.org.uk

National Centre for Learning and Literacy
The University of Reading
Bulmershe Court
Reading, RG6 1HY
www.ncll.reading.ac.uk

National Council on Intellectual Disability
PO Box 771
Mawson
ACT 2607
Australia
www.dice.org.au

Index

This edition 2004

Franklin Watts
96 Leonard Street
London
EC2A 4XD

Franklin Watts Australia
45-51 Huntley Street
Alexandria
NSW 2015

Copyright © 2000

ISBN: 0 7496 5584 4

Dewey Decimal Classification
Number: 362.4

10 9 8 7 6 5 4 3 2 1

A CIP catalogue record for
this book is available from the
British Library.

Printed in Malaysia

Consultants: The Down's Syndrome
Association; Beverley Mathias, REACH.
Editor: Samantha Armstrong
Designer: Louise Snowdon
Photographer: Chris Fairclough
except P18-9 from Express Syndication
Illustrator: Derek Matthews

With thanks to: Cherry Moore, Sue Marshall,
Gael and Michael Reeve, South East Derbyshire
College and The Daily Express.